Through the Tunnel to Win the Heart

The story about a USAID nurse of faith in Vietnam

Nancy M. Churchill

ISBN 978-1-64559-315-7 (Paperback)
ISBN 978-1-64559-316-4 (Digital)

Copyright © 2019 Nancy M. Churchill
All rights reserved
First Edition

THE WEIGHT OF GLORY by C.S. Lewis
©C.S. Lewis Pte. Ltd. 1949
THE SCREWTAPE LETTERS by C.S. Lewis
©C.S. Lewis Pte. Ltd. 1942
Permission from the estate of C.S. Lewis.

In this book the name of an individual may be changed in places.

All rights reserved. No part of this publication may be reproduced, distributed, or transmitted in any form or by any means, including photocopying, recording, or other electronic or mechanical methods without the prior written permission of the publisher. For permission requests, solicit the publisher via the address below.

Covenant Books, Inc.
11661 Hwy 707
Murrells Inlet, SC 29576
www.covenantbooks.com

This book is dedicated to a dear friend in war,
"Ginny"
Virginia A. Humphrey Snip
July 12, 1932–March 1, 2018

Map used with permission.

Contents

1. "[Her Parents] Did Not Know It Was of the Lord" (Judges 14:4) 7
2. Orientation: Washington, D.C. 10
3. In Country 12
4. Gone: The Ignorance of War 18
5. Nepal 21
6. The High Price of War 24
7. Christmas and More 28
8. TET 1968 46
9. My Tho 56
10. Return to Phu Vinh 67
11. Mini TET 74
12. The Long Way Home 79
Epilogue 85
The Ellison Children 87
Acknowledgments 89
Glossary 91

CHAPTER 1

"[Her Parents] Did Not Know It Was of the Lord" (Judges 14:4)

My parents took me to the airport. It was an early-morning flight from Syracuse, New York, to Washington, D.C., a beautiful October day in 1966. Just four months ago I had come home from Mwanza, Tanzania, in the Peace Corps, and now I had a meeting this morning at the U.S. Agency for International Development (AID) at the State Department.

I sat across the desk from this attractive gray-haired lady. She was busy gathering information from me and endlessly writing it all down. Then she stopped, looked up, and said, "We need nurses in Vietnam!" then returned to writing. But I had other ideas.

"Don't you need nurses in India or Pakistan?" I asked.

She was absorbed in paperwork, not listening. I leaned forward. "Don't you need nurses in India or Pakistan?"

Her answer was quick and short. "No! Go to the room at the end of the hall and take a language aptitude test."

Language? Aptitude? I have none! I took two years of Latin in four. My excellent teacher, Mrs. Brown, miraculously squeezed out a passing regent's grade of 65 the second time around. I needed it for nursing school.

I entered the room at the end of the hall. The young man gave instructions. I was surprisingly calm. Finished! He corrected it right then. "Well, you passed by two points," he said, sounding less than thrilled, but I was exuberant. Gleefully, I walked back up the hall and returned to the desk.

"I passed the test," I blurted out.

"Many don't," she replied.

Now it was 12 o'clock, lunchtime; still more paperwork to do. The offices closed, and everyone departed for dining rooms and cafeterias. But I was directed to the basement near the loading dock where vending machines of food and drink were located. As I sat eating my archaic sandwich, what my mother had said to me at the airport that morning kept echoing in my mind, "Don't let anyone send you to Vietnam."

I walked out onto the loading dock and stood in silence in the fresh air. At that moment I knew this was where my Savior wanted me to go.

I walked back up to the desk. All the paperwork was completed, and I was told AID would notify me when to come to Washington for training in area studies and language.

The flight home was on time. As I got into the driver's seat, the first words Mom said to me were "Where are they sending you?"

"Vietnam," I replied.

"Your father is going to be hurt! You'll have to tell him! I'm not going to!"

Some years ago, I realized I had the most wonderful parents in the whole world. This hurt, fear, and anger in her voice was new to me.

What had I done! The thought of telling my father became unbearable. Was he home from work yet? I thought. We rode the rest of the way home in silence as the unusually bright and beautiful fall colors flashed by.

His car was in the driveway. He's home!

"Where are they sending you?" His first words were the same as my mother's.

"I don't know yet," I blurted out in fear, without thought.

My brother had enlisted in the Coast Guard Reserve for eight years in December 1952 at seventeen while still in high school. Mom and Dad may have accepted that their son could possibly be in a war, but certainly not their daughter.

As Thanksgiving, Christmas, and New Year's came and went, I was so happy my dad did not know yet that I was going to Vietnam. My mother looked at me. "Nancy, when are you going to tell him? When you're getting on the plane?"

I had no reply. I still couldn't face telling him.

In late January my mom did tell my dad I was going to Vietnam. We never discussed it. We both knew it would hurt too much.

CHAPTER 2

Orientation: Washington, D.C.

As the taxi pulled up in front of the hotel on February 12, 1967—Lincoln's birthday—I stepped out into slush. Washington, I thought, is somewhere between winter and spring, and it doesn't know which.

The cockroaches in my room were tiny, transparent little things; not like the ones in Tanzania, the size of my thumb, when I was there in the Peace Corps. Their favorite place was in the bathroom and specifically on the toilet paper. I never knew why.

In the morning I went over to the State Department early and found the room we were to meet in locked. I was the first to arrive.

Then came Virginia "Ginny" Humphrey, tall and slender. We had a while to talk. She had grown up on a farm in Oklahoma and had been a missionary in Egypt.

I thought, how wonderful, another Christian, a mature Christian. I was a fairly new Christian. I had come to faith in Christ and His Word in Tanzania.

We were friends from the start!

Three days a week, we were put on a bus for language study in Arlington taught by Vietnamese. The other two days were spent in area studies a few blocks from the apartment.

Although there were eighty in our group, perhaps twelve were nurses, and the rest were all going to Vietnam to work on a multitude of different projects.

On Sundays Ginny and I went to church, then to dinner and discussed the sermon

She loved to sew and made many of her clothes We'd go to the shopping district looking for fabric, but I was usually the one that spent the most money.

Ginny had taken a course in college in How to Learn a Second Language, and she was good. And as good as she was, I was equivalently poor.

Nevertheless, many evenings she'd come by my apartment and "drag" me to the language lab at State, where we, alone, would put on the headphones and listen to Vietnamese and I'd suffer.

"We're all sitting around too much and not getting enough exercise," Ginny announced one day, "so let's play softball."

"Softball?" I hadn't played softball since grade school, and I'm sure the other nurses hadn't either.

"And we can ask our Vietnamese language instructors if they would like to play," she said enthusiastically.

"Ginny, they probably never heard of softball." I was right, they hadn't. Nevertheless, since I lived closest to Washington, I called Mom and Dad and asked them to send a softball, catcher's mitt, and bat. So began the most fun I had in Washington.

The baseball diamond was near the mall. I don't know how much exercise we got, but I sure did laugh. We performed like clowns in a circus, loving every minute of it!

This site became the location for the Vietnam Veterans Memorial in 1982.

CHAPTER 3

In Country

People were called up unexpectedly, on purpose. Instead of going to class, all the nurses in our group met in another room. We were given our passports, plane tickets, and told we had five days' Leave. Goodbye! Like shipments of goods to the Front.

Memorial Day weekend was a wonderful time to be home. One of the days was spent at Eighth Lake in the Adirondacks, where we had camped every year since 1943 when I was five years old.

Then on June 5, there was not much talk at the airport. We hugged; I turned, walked out, got on the plane, and was gone.

Ginny and I would meet up in Los Angeles and fly together to the other side of the world.

I called home from LA Airport. I could only talk to Mom. Dad was upset, she said, and she had sent him out for a walk. On their way home from the airport, Dad had stopped to return something to Sack's department store. My family had known the Sack family all our lives. He told Milly Sack he had just dropped me off at the airport to go to Vietnam. She cried. Dad hurried out of the store before his tears were visible.

We refueled in Honolulu and Guam, then went on to Saigon. The door opened; the ramp placed. The oppressive heat poured in over us. With throngs of people, we had to weave in, out, and around to make our way to the terminal.

AID personnel picked us up and dropped us at the Excelsior Hotel. I noticed scurrying around Saigon were rats so huge we could have hosted "The Run of the Bulls" up Tu Do Street with the frenzied balls of teeth and tails.

Then we started six days of orientation, lots of paperwork, a tour of Cho Ray Hospital, a briefing in a vault, and a party held on the roof where Ginny and I met John, who worked for the American Embassy. We both liked him immediately, and he knew it. He invited us out to dinner one evening

We would see him again.

Several of us boarded a C47 for Can Tho, which was regional headquarters for the Mekong Delta that included most all the land south of Saigon. Everyone left the next day for other places, except Ginny and me.

Lynn Kelly, who was supervisor for all the AID nurses in the Delta, took us on a tour of the hospital. We observed in the clinic a young boy riddled with shrapnel. I thought I was going to vomit. I turned and walked to the front of the room. Right then I was determined that would not happen again.

The next day I had dysentery, which was to plague me off and on throughout my tour.

After six days in Can Tho, Ginny and I flew on to Phu Vinh, Vinh Binh Province, where we would spend the rest of our tour.

Two Christians in a war together! This was God ordained!

Vinh Binh Province was located between the Ba Sac and the Co Chien rivers, the two main branches of the Mekong. The province is militarily very active since the Viet Cong (VC) wanted control of the rivers that led into the South China Sea.

The province consists of seven districts, and the largest town is Phu Vinh, where the one hospital was located.

Our "quarters" consisted of a large single-story house with a living room/dining room, open and together with floor tiles that didn't mix or match. In the back was a large screened-in kitchen with a cistern under the floor and a holding tank on the roof. Four bedrooms and a bath were in line along the right side. The living room was comfortable with a sofa, chairs, and an enormous ottoman. A small screened-in porch led down three steps to the driveway. Next was a fence with a door size cut-out leading to a pre-fab ranch house. Four air force doctors lived there: two surgeons, Bob Leonard, team leader, and Bud McDougal; a pediatrician, Steve Dickstein, and a medical doctor, Lottie Varano.

Every one of the forty-four provinces in South Vietnam had a civilian hospital, and as many provinces as possible had Americans assigned to it. They could be military, civilian, or mixed, consisting of doctors, an administrator, corpsmen, or medics and nurses. The military name for this group was called "The Milphap Team."

After rest and unpacking, Ong Sang, chief nurse, took Ginny and me on a tour of the hospital. A six-foot-high wall encompassed the compound, except for one entrance with a large guardhouse. On the right was the maternity ward, lab, and a small supply building. Everything else was to the left. Every ward was a separate building connected by a walkway.

Then we toured the OR, the only building screen-enclosed that I could see. We went down a short hallway to a large open area; to the right was the recovery room and an operating room. On the left a second operating room, central service, a small supply closet, and a tiny room just wide enough for a toilet where an unlikely door to the outside had been cut into the wall, I believe, as an escape.

That evening we attended a briefing at MACV (Military Assistance Command Vietnam) and were introduced to around sixty army personnel. They were to become very kind and important to us.

In the morning we went to work, June 23; Ginny to the OR, I to pediatrics. I walked slowly through the ward. Thirty beds, adult size, with a mat covering the planks. I first noticed the glass IV bottles. The tubing was covered with flies. I looked closer. What's in there? Bugs floating on top! The bottle was so designed that when the rubber seal was removed, a glass rod the size of a straw, acting as the air vent, allowed the bugs to climb into the bottle, feasting on glucose—that sugary substance—allowing some to drip onto the tubing when the bottle was inverted to hang.

I found new bottles, removed the seal, placed adhesive tape over the air vent, and stuck a 14-gauge needle through it for the vent. It wasn't perfectly sealed, but that was all I could think to do.

As I continued my walk, I noticed a little girl, her abdomen open. I could see all her organs. Her mother was by her side, continuously fanning to keep the flies out. I would remember the agony always.

I wasn't here to 'take over" a job but rather do a much-needed job.

Co Thu was head nurse, an excellent one at that. She was an expert in starting IVs on children, and she spoke English very well.

The nurses' station was at one end of the ward, and to the left of that was a side room, with a table suitable for wound care. I asked and no one person was working there regularly. I would like to do that.

I set up a dressing cart with sterile canisters of 4 x 4's and ABD pads, transfer forceps, hemostats in alcohol, and normal saline. I could do wound care, one after the other, with a minimum of cross-contamination. Cleaning the wound first was paramount. I mixed Phisohex and peroxide and diluted it with normal saline, and with sterile cotton balls, held with a hemostat, I could really clean a wound well. There were no gloves. To keep the flies and filth out, every wound had to be covered well.

I needed something to keep the dressings from sticking to burns. Dr. Leonard came up with the answer: a jar of water-soluble cream, one ounce of silver nitrate crystals, and a bottle of tetracycline, mixed. It reduced infection and promoted healing.

A week later another nurse arrived, Sheila Johnson, and she was willing to work in the operating room, much to Ginny's delight. We both liked awake patients to interact with. This was where the three of us would work for the duration of our tour in Vietnam, which was eighteen months.

Since we weren't allowed to walk anywhere for safety concerns, we were given an international scout to drive. We worked five and a half days a week, leaving Saturday at noon. Rarely did we return on Sunday unless for an emergency. However, we would go to the orphanage on Saturday afternoon sometimes. The very young and toddlers were the most vulnerable. We could walk over, as it was just behind the hospital. The nuns ran it. I think Dr. Dickstein really liked working there. I liked holding the babies that needed so much to be held, which they weren't used to. When I would begin to hold the little one, she would become rigid, not quite knowing what this strange feeling was, but then I would feel the baby relax and then be comforted.

Lt. Colonel Schowalter was commander of Vinh Binh Province along with the Vietnamese counterpart. He was very experienced, an excellent leader. He was interested in everyone's job. He was given a great deal of respect. In a few months he would be transferred to a much larger town, a place called My Tho.

Lt. Colonel Girdner would take over. He too was very experienced and was well liked and respected also.

Then there was Captain Hank Baver, administrator of the hospital, the go-to guy for all hospital needs and everything else. Hank saw humor in everyday life all the time. We were too small a group for Bob Hope to visit, but we had Hank.

Being civilian nurses, anyone and everyone could come to our house for talk, singing, pizza, dinner, or an after-church brunch; officers with enlisted. Just the right balance and yet our privacy was respected. I soon learned it didn't take much of an excuse to have a party.

On July 4, Vinh Long, our near neighbor upriver, had a change-of-command party. Liz, an AID nurse, invited all the nurses in the Delta to come.

The party was held in a hangar with hundreds of military. This was headquarters for two helicopter groups: The "Outlaws" that mainly flew troops in and out of battle, and the "Mavericks" that flew gunships carrying rockets in aggressive action.

Liz had her living room turned into a dormitory for the night. The party's over! Back to Phu Vinh!

We were mortared two to three times a week, usually over the weekend, sometime between 11 p.m. and 5 a.m. The doctors came over with helmets, flak jackets, and guns. I made breakfast once, but making coffee became routine.

We had been told to get on the floor and pull the mattress over us. Who needs it! I had to work in the morning and needed sleep.

The plaster would fall, the bed would collapse, once simultaneously but unrelated.

We got word a battalion of VC were to attack Phu Vinh. As it turned out, the gunships eliminated the threat before they reached us.

After this we were taken out to a rice paddy. Major White, commander of Phu Vinh, thought we should learn to shoot and be given guns. Target practice! Sheila chose a 45-caliber pistol. I chose the MI Carbine. Ginny didn't take a gun. I took the gun because my concern was that I'd get separated and some young soldier would work his way to rescue me, costing him his own life. I didn't want that to happen. I wanted to defend myself. I also knew if it came to that, it was over!

To complete our instruction this day, the major thought we needed to know the full history of the grenade. He pulled the pin. We three hit the dirt in fetal position, waiting to be blown up, as he kept talking and holding the thing. We didn't know it had to be thrown, releasing the handle for it to detonate, which he did… finally!

CHAPTER 4

Gone: The Ignorance of War

On Sundays, chaplains were "choppered" from place to place around the Delta holding services in all the provinces. One Catholic, one Protestant. Ginny and I went over to MACV a couple of times. However, we always went to the Tin-Lanh Church down by the runway. The service, being in Vietnamese, I read my Bible. There were fifteen present. Most Vietnamese are either Buddhist or Catholic.

Pastor Diep and his wife invited us to their house, next to the church, after services. The lead interpreter at the hospital, Ong Phuoc, and his wife came along to help in communication. Their house was full of young people. They had nine children; the youngest was thirteen. Soon we all were given tea and "Pop-Tarts." The tea was good!

Pastor Diep told us American missionaries were coming to Phu Vinh soon and that they had been missionaries in Cambodia. (A third of Phu Vinh is Cambodian.)

For some reason, I thought they wouldn't come. It was too good to be true!

A week later, on September 3, the pastor and his wife were coming back home from My Tho on their motor bike when they were ambushed by a group of VC. He was not hurt. They killed her. The mother of nine. Why?

Senseless, waste, meaningless, confusing!

She was buried behind the church in mud. The rainy season had started!

So many wounded—and the children. There was no end! No let-up! I prayed fervently, asking God to change the war. "Please, God, less wounded." Nothing changed. It would not stop. Day after day, the same pain, torn bodies. Couldn't He do something?

Then I'll change it! I can do it. Fasting! That's it. God would answer my prayers for the war to improve if I'd just fast. I'll take control! Now I can handle anything—wounded children—all of it!

But the war didn't change. It got worse.

And it was to get a lot worse!

There I was slipping down into a "works" faith, my biblical ignorance leading the way.

The missionaries did come. Paul and Eunice Ellison with their daughter, Linda, who was four years old. They had three other children in the Dalat MK School at Tanah Rata in Cameron Highlands, Malaysia: Elaine, fourteen; David, twelve, and Bobby, eight. They would be home on vacation soon.

As far as I was concerned, they were heaven sent—for me. They were the stability, peace, and love I needed.

Am I overstating it? No. They were all of that and more to me. I knew I'd love them forever!

Ginny and I were given the privilege of watching Linda in the afternoon sometimes when Paul and Eunice had meetings to attend. She was the most happy, smart, and beautiful little girl I had ever met. What fun I had playing with her—making clay animals and stuff.

Paul told us one day of growing up in Phnom Penh, Cambodia, where his parents had been missionaries.

The family had just arrived in Bangkok, Thailand, after a year's furlough in the States.

It was December 7, 1941. The Japanese, having posed as civilians, then put on uniforms and took over everything. The family was sent to a detention camp. The Japanese had better things to do than guard a bunch of missionaries and other civilians, so the camp was turned over to the Thai people. Food was scarce, so Paul, then twelve at the time, would sneak out of camp in the night and scavenge for food.

In 1943 an exchange was made. By then Paul weighed 120 pounds and was over six feet tall.

He remembers being taken to a port, walking along on the far side of the train, seeing between the cars Japanese crying, clinging to the rail as they were pulled from the ship.

The exchange made, they returned to the States until the end of the war.

CHAPTER 5

Nepal

John, from the US Embassy in Saigon, came down to Phu Vinh for a visit and brought Marie Law, who I'd met in Saigon during orientation. She mentioned that Ambassador Bunker flew to Nepal every six weeks to visit his wife, who was ambassador there and that we could try and get our name on the flight manifest and take R&R for six days.

It worked! The embassy called and Marie and I were off to Katmandu.

The mountains loomed over us in the near distance, luring us to come closer. We found a driver and a Land Rover, driving twelve miles up into the mist. Such peace! Such beauty!

A couple invited us to a Nepalese home for a delicious chicken dinner. They planned on crossing over into China, which was a concern to me.

In the morning I got up before sunrise. Katmandu below was blanketed in clouds. And then suddenly the sky lit up, the first rays of sun hit the highest peaks, slowly cascading down the mountains as if God was pouring liquid gold from His hand over them.

As the temperature rose and warmed the air, the clouds lifted over Katmandu, and by mid-afternoon the mountains were obscured from view.

The next day, walking down the twelve miles to Katmandu, we saw life peaceful and full of joy, or was it I full of joy, as men and boys carried loads of wood on their backs up the mountain. Families herding goats and sheep to new pastures. Small villages full of activity. People smiled and waved as we passed by. No foot mines here!

The next day we rested by the pool.

Everyone was already on the plane when the ambassador and his wife arrived. He boarded and went forward to his cabin without a word, not like the greeting he gave to us as he boarded leaving Vietnam.

As we entered Vietnam air space, everyone was quiet with their own thoughts the rest of the way into Saigon.

From mortar attacks over the weekends, the casualties were waiting for us. Ginny and I went to the recovery room where the wounded were waiting for surgery.

I noticed a man sitting in the corner; his turban caked in blood got my attention. His scalp was open across the top down to the skull with embedded dirt so thick it took a medic and me some time to clean it.

Next, a young girl, her hair matted with blood, and under this, a large piece of shrapnel anchored to her skull, saving her brain. Dr. Leonard was able to remove it and she was fine. I thought how miraculous some wounds were.

I could tell when Co Thu would come on the ward and was having a tough time facing wounded children. I wanted to help her, and yet, I also could hardly face a new day sometimes. Maybe if we could talk but not at work. I invited her to dinner to talk and play Parcheesi—Ginny always won! Oh well, we just had to get used to it!

Co Thu came several times to dinner, and it helped her and me both.

The hospital grounds looked like a barnyard: there were cows, goats, geese, dogs and lots of pigs. Finally, it was decided to put a gate at the entrance; though holes in the wall, roundabout, could continue to accommodate some of the beasts.

But there was one little bitty animal you could never keep out and that was the ever-present cockroach.

I tried never to underestimate the creativity and ingenuity of children. At the hospital, the young boys would build a tiny wooden cart and then tie a string on the front, grab a squiggling roach (a talent in itself), slip the string under its small wings, and let it go! Down the walkway, weaving side to side, the roach ran with great speed in a frenzy, trying to rid itself from what was chasing it. The race was on!

Who would have ever thought the filthy little thing could be so funny.

CHAPTER 6

The High Price of War

On November 8 a conference was held in Can Tho. All the nurses in the Delta were to attend.

The chief American civilian for the Delta spoke: "The war is won in the Delta. The ARVN troops don't realize they are on the offensive. We have to encourage them, but the war is won here!"

Well, you sure could have fooled me. Isn't that nice to hear that the war is won. And just think, I still thought the war hadn't changed, not one little bit—with all the wounded and mortar attacks ongoing. How wrong could I be!

And this gentleman spoke to congressmen when they came here on their "fact-finding tour."

In a few short weeks he would find out just how "won the war" really was!

In November Paul had gone to Saigon to pick up Elaine, David, and Bobby from school. They would have their long vacation now lasting until almost the end of January.

By mid-November we had lost at least four Americans in Phu Vinh. The exact number I do not know. I am not going to talk about the loss because I feel it is private and belongs only to the families.

I had decided to put an end to my biblical ignorance. Perhaps there was an answer to all this human destruction in His Word. I'd devour the New Testament, then continue onto the rest.

I soon reached Matthew 21:22, "And all things, whatsoever ye shall ask in prayer, believing, ye shall receive." Anything? It probably should be asked in God's will, not my will. Was it God's will for the war to improve when the war was man-made in evil and hate? The more I had prayed for the war to improve, it didn't!

Then I read in John 16:33, Jesus said: "In the world ye shall have tribulation: but be of good cheer; I have overcome the world."

How then should I pray? John 13:34 said: "We are to love one another as Jesus loves us." Then James 5:16 told me to "pray for one another."

I would then pray for everyone I knew in Phu Vinh. They were easy to pray for because I loved them. We had a wonderful group of people. So wonderful that an army doctor would come to Phu Vinh for R&R once in a while to be with people who cared for each other.

In the evening I would sometimes sit on the porch steps and listen to the "night sounds": peaceful muffled voices near, a dog barking in the distance, and right on time, the soup man clicking bowls together as he passed by, never seen in the darkness.

But tonight! Tonight, there were no sounds!

Ginny came out on the porch and stood behind the screen door.

"Listen," I said, "it's so quiet."

Then heavy gunfire, coming from the end of the street. We moved in unison. The screen door, so easy to open, was now like trying to open a vault. Ginny hit the electric converter switch just inside the door. Everything went black. She tripped and fell on top of the ottoman, both being propelled into the dining room. I laughed so hard I nearly fell over; then incoming mortar cut short the laughter.

The doctors would be over soon!

The Friday before Thanksgiving I was returning from Saigon on an Air America plane. As we approached Phu Vinh, the runway looked deserted.

A CIA man ran to the plane, grabbed me off, and we sped away in his jeep.

"What's wrong?" I asked.

"The officer that took Major White's place was ambushed and killed this morning. The VC are all around, mostly just south of the runway."

As we pulled into the driveway, "chopper" gunships had already begun air strikes where we had just come from. More gunships were vibrating overhead.

The next morning a jet was called in from Cam Ranh Bay. We were all standing in the driveway watching from three blocks away as the jet climbed and climbed then with full power screamed in a dive that I could feel up my spine, dropping its ordinance on its target of VC.

After church on Sunday, Sheila and I went to the Ellisons for dinner. It was a happy time with all the kids home. Ginny was on R&R in Malaysia.

Again, this day the jet continued air strikes. Later in the afternoon we returned home. The air strikes had stopped. The relaxing quiet was welcome.

Soon some of the men from MACV started to filter into the living room, caked in mud. The doctors came over. A great sadness, with a need to be together, filled the room. Something was wrong. I could see it on their faces.

One of the officers started to talk in a tone as if he was giving an official report, perhaps to hide his true feelings. He looked down at the mud drying on his boots and spoke slowly, hardly audible.

"We think we killed most of the VC that caused the ambush Friday. There was either missed communication or a wind change when the smoke flare was released. We aren't sure. The pilot said he was running low on fuel and this would be his last run and would unload everything. The hit was close to the American and ARVN troops killing several."

One of the doctors spoke up, "A wounded American lay nearby and said 'I can't leave my kids. Please don't let me die!' He died before the chopper could pick him up."

By now it was long past the supper hour at MACV. Nobody cared. No one wanted to leave. There was comfort together here. A special love for one another that defies explanation. I felt God's presence that evening in that room. Everyone stayed until 1:00 a.m. I'll never forget it.

Four more VC battalions were surrounding the town by Tuesday. They were supposed to attack that night but didn't. Perhaps the air strikes changed their mind.

Finally, Thanksgiving Day! In the morning, at our house, everyone was invited over for breakfast. Dinner was at 1 p.m. at MACV in the briefing room. A turkey dinner with everything was served, and it was the best. Most all the men wore civilian clothes and that was as close to home as they would get. I felt joy mixed with quiet sadness.

The next two days were very busy with a large increase in casualties. It never stops! Never!

A child was found to have diphtheria, so we then vaccinated all the children on the ward.

At 5 a.m. Sunday the VC mortared the town so heavily that I finally did what I had been told to do and I got under the mattress.

Now the ante had been raised! By daybreak B52s were called in from Cam Ranh Bay. There was no more trouble with the VC for a while after that, except for the usual weekend mortars.

That afternoon we went to MACV for a memorial service for those no longer with us.

CHAPTER 7

Christmas and More

C. S. Lewis[1] wrote: "I believe Christianity as I believe that the Sun has risen, not only because I see it, but because I see everything else."

Now I had something else to deal with. Drinking! I had always felt "social" drinking was fine for a Christian as long as it wasn't taken to drunkenness. I was drinking more than I liked, and if I wanted to see where I was headed, all I had to do was look around and not too far. I did not want to go home an alcoholic!

I looked at Ginny. She never drank. She just would say, "No, thank you," like a broken record over and over, then finally no one would ask her anymore and she didn't have to make a decision as to how much! That seemed so much easier—just become a broken record. I stopped for life on December 7—an easy day to remember.

A week later I realized drinking was not a good testimony for a Christian. Then I saw in I Corinthians 8:9, "But take heed lest by any means this liberty of yours become a stumbling block to them that are weak." Even though this verse speaks about eating meat from idols, I feel it can also have a broader meaning: not to promote or encourage others to become alcoholics.

ARVN troops were now assigned to guard us at the house. They would be staying in the garage out back.

---

[1] C. S. Lewis, "The Weight of Glory" (page 92).

The policy was to "pacify" each hamlet. Our government thought they would have pacified enough hamlets by 1970 to make South Vietnam secure. My thought was it would take at least until 1978, and that meant a very long war that I didn't think my country would tolerate. How wrong we both were.

Twice before I had been away from home for Christmas and I had found it actually to be enjoyable. This Christmas was very different. I desperately longed to be home. We all did! But that was about to change.

The Ellisons had us over for dinner before Christmas, and it was such fun with the family. Paul showed us the dollhouse he had made for Linda. All the rooms were decorated and furnished beautifully. So much work. He said, "This will give Linda a lot of playtime."

This Christmas eve the Tin-Lanh church was packed to overflowing. Hank Baver, Dr. Dickstein, and Dr. Leonard, the three of us, and of course, the Ellisons got up on the platform and sang "Joy to the World" to a sea of faces that I have never forgotten.

Christmas morning the doctors, with Hank dressed as Santa Claus, went to the orphanage to pass out presents to all the children. Dr. Leonard's wife had sent the gifts given by their church. There were mountains of stuffed animals the children could hold to themselves in comfort.

Hank was then driven all around Phu Vinh in that red suit. I would have loved to know what the Vietnamese were thinking about these crazy Americans.

As we ate Christmas dinner at MACV, a plane flew overhead playing Christmas carols. Today there was peace!

Christmas was over! That night we had incoming mortar!

A Cambodian girl on the ward had lost her leg when she stepped on a foot mine. She was the most unkempt child I had seen. Her clothes were rotten and falling off, and her hair was matted with lice. She finally allowed me to cut her hair and get rid of the lice. I was very fond of her. She was smart with unusual wisdom for her age. I rummaged through a box of clothes Hank had in his office and found pants and a checkered red-and-white blouse that she never took off.

I would often wonder what the children grew up to be. How much more suffering? Did they have a family and find peace and joy in their lives? Did a missionary like Paul (and Eunice) lead them to the Lord in what was to become a highly restricted country?

Steve Dickstein wanted a New Year's Eve party at our house for all the Vietnamese we worked with at the hospital. Invitations were given out, decorations made, food and drink secured. MACV was also invited.

The party was to start around 8:00 p.m. They must have read the invitation wrong since they started arriving at noon. Oh well, we were prepared! So we thought! Firecrackers were hung on the wall and lit. Throngs of people came in like a stampede. We surrendered and gave up at 4 a.m. and went to bed. The party didn't "give up" until 6 a.m. Little did we know we hadn't seen anything yet.

Pediatric building

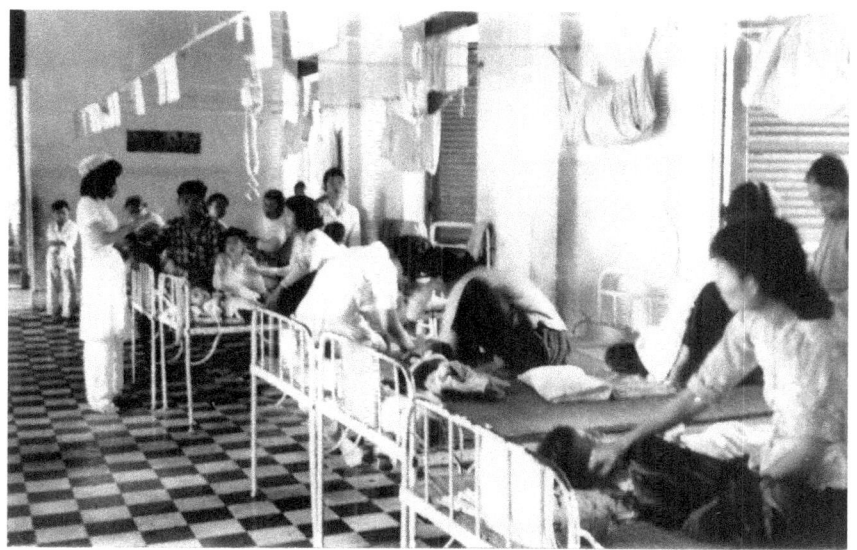
Pediatric ward

The room for wound care

Some children on ward standing on walkway

THROUGH THE TUNNEL TO WIN THE HEART

Two friends on ward

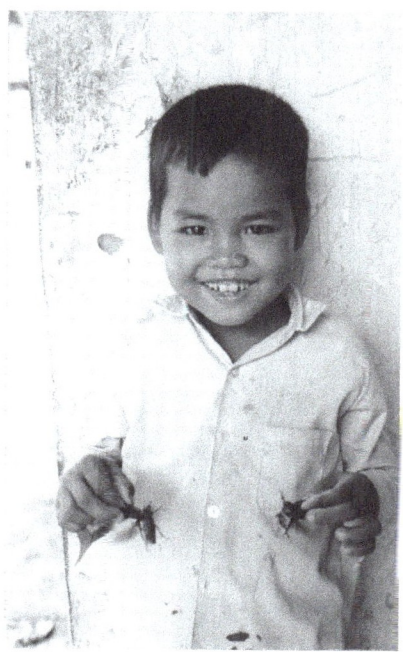

Boy holding cockroaches

Nancy and Ginny on firing range

Nancy and Co Thu, Head Nurse Pediatrics

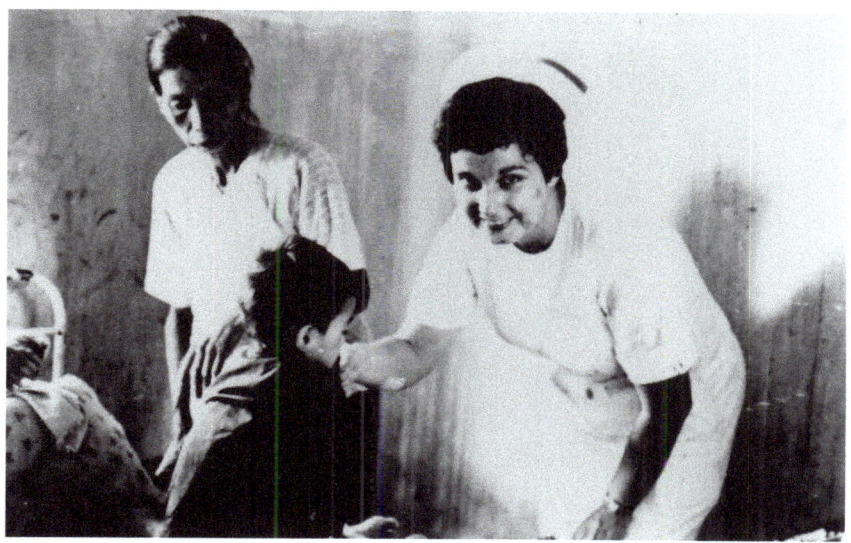
Nancy on Pediatrics

Dr. Steve Dickstein on ward

Lt. Col. Ralph Girdner

Dr. Bob Leonard

Dr Bud McDougal and Ong Liem

Capt. Hank Baver with children

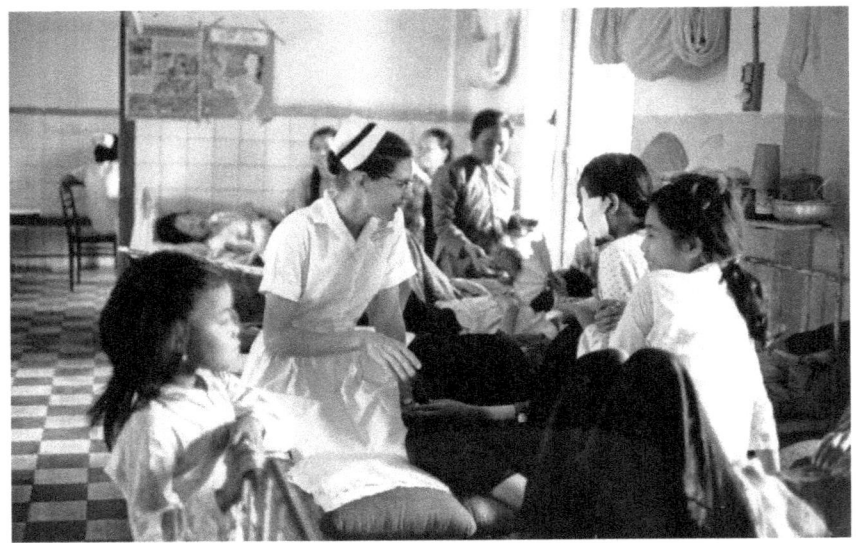
Ginny on women's surgical ward

Paul and Eunice Ellison with children Elaine, Bobby, Linda, and David

Eunice, Paul, and Linda with Jambi

Linda on Bobby's bike

Tin-Lanh Church with Pastor Diep, Paul, and Ginny

Toddlers at orphanage

THROUGH THE TUNNEL TO WIN THE HEART

Nancy in Nepal

Capt. Hank Baver as Santa

Christmas at orphanage, laughing at Santa

Dr. Varano, Ginny, and Dr. Dickstein at MACV
on first day of TET Offensive

Nancy at Navy compound in My Tho

Young child comforting baby in My Tho

Wedding of Ong Duc and Co Ha

Linda, Co Thu, and Dr. Dickstein

CHAPTER 8

TET 1968

The Vietnamese New Year is the grandest of all their holidays; it is called TET. Celebrations start a week or more before with gatherings of family and friends with endless parties. Depending on the phase of the moon, this year TET was January 30. At that time all the Vietnamese become a year older.

It is very important for all Vietnamese to be home with their families at this time and the North Vietnamese Army and the VC know this!

Wednesday, January 31, 3:20 a.m. Incoming mortar! I sat bolt upright in bed. I listened: hard, heavy nonstop shelling. My heart pounding, ready to take flight from my chest, I dove to the floor, taking the mattress with me.

Heavy, running footsteps came into the living room. Then whispering, always whispering at first as if the VC might hear.

I stayed where I was. Why was I so frightened this time?

"Heavenly Father," I prayed, "in Your Word you have promised anything asked in prayer, believing I can receive. Lord, I am asking now and believe You will keep us all safe—Paul, Eunice, and Linda, the doctors, Ginny, Sheila, and me and all the men at MACV and our friends at the hospital. Thank you, Jesus!"

Immediately a calm came over me. I was again five years old, and my mother had just tucked me into bed. Peace filled me that was God-given. I fell asleep.

At daybreak I heard a plane fly overhead, then it was gone. Sheila came into my room and said they were bringing wounded to the doctors' house. This time the shelling didn't stop at sunrise. I squirmed out from under the mattress; by now it felt like the roof was on top of me. I got dressed, but this time in fatigues.

Small-arms fire was intense and everywhere. Three wounded Vietnamese soldiers were already at the doctors' house when we got there.

Tom Hayden came in with a superficial neck wound, and Colonel Girdner came with him. Tom headed up the USAID office here, which in Vietnam is called CORDS.

Colonel Girdner then related what happened: "There was a blast at the CORDS office. Then the VC shot the five Vietnamese guards. Then another blast nearby, when they blew the front door off of the province chief's house. All the family ran out the back and made it safely to MACV." The colonel then left.

A gunship was delivering air strikes overhead then it was gone. Another wounded American came with shrapnel in his back. Dr. Leonard, with Dr. McDougal, had made it to the hospital under fire and returned with supplies. All were treated and taken out to MACV temporarily.

Next came word a CIA agent had been shot in the abdomen near the hospital. Dr. Leonard again left and made it to the hospital where they had taken him. He got him stabilized and onto a chopper where they both flew to Dong Tham Evac. Center. Dr. Leonard returned to Phu Vinh later that day. The agent recovered and returned in three weeks.

Dr. Varano and Dr. Dickstein and the three of us sat in the living room in silence. Dr. Dickstein had the radio on trying to get information. Are we the only town under attack?

The calm that was given as a gift from the Lord last night was still with me. I was there and yet not caught up in it.

The morning was almost gone. We moved to the bunker between the houses that had been taken over by mosquitos, then back to the living room, not knowing where we wanted to be nor should be. The surgeons were either at the hospital or trying to get there.

A Vietnamese policeman came into the house and announced in broken English, "You go to hospital now. VC left town!"

Sheila walked back to the kitchen, and I heard the bolt in the lock as she slammed the door to her bedroom.

I grabbed my Ml Carbine and the belt filled with clips of ammunition. Dr. Varano and Dr. Dickstein gathered their rifles. Soldiers were all around the house. Sheila was not alone. Ginny was through the front door already.

We only got to the curb when Hank Baver pulled up in a Scout.

"Where do you think you're going? Get in! I'll take you to the hospital. You can't walk. The VC are all over the place."

"What's the matter, Hank? You look terrible," I said while getting in.

The Scout pulled out down the back way. Hank went on, breathless, "The colonel sent me out to get a VC body count. Smoke was still coming out of them. I was trapped behind this building for a while, then I just ran for it and got picked up."

We shot through the entrance! Everyone leaped out and ran into the operating room. Ginny finished triage with Dr. Varano and Dr. Dickstein while I set up a dressing cart. The surgeons had just begun operating.

Several wounded ARVN soldiers were lying in the walkway by the emergency room. Ginny and I headed over with the dressing cart. I put the gun down and we went to work. Their wounds were not life threatening. Firing continued around us. Sweat was pouring off me in buckets. We finished!

Ginny said she wanted to check on a lady with an ostomy. I didn't feel good about her leaving, but we didn't interfere with each other!

I picked up the gun and started back to the OR. The firing was closer and louder. I dropped to my knees crawling, pushing the dressing cart ahead.

I started to laugh. In nursing school, I could hear our director of nursing say, as she had many times over, "This is *not* nursing!"

Ten feet from the screen door to the OR, I made a right turn. Lying on either side of the walkway were two soldiers. "Nancy, what are you doing here?"

My brain had stopped. I responded as an automaton, "What are you doing here?"

Standing behind the screen door was a CIA agent wearing what was called black pajamas. Hanging from his neck was a very small, very powerful rifle with a very long clip in place. "You're getting out of here *now*!"

I'm not going anywhere without Ginny! I backed up on all fours, looking down the walkway. There she is! Coming, walking like she's on a stroll in the park. I motioned for her to get down. When she reached me, I stood up, pushing the cart through the screen door, the agent in the lead. We ran into the OR, then through the escape door, running so fast it felt like flight. We got to the jeep parked by the side of the guardhouse. The sergeant in the driver's seat motioned for us to get in. Dr. Varano was already there, then he left and returned with Dr. Dickstein.

I sat on the floor behind the driver. Dr. Dickstein sat next to me. Dr. Varano sat in the front passenger seat, and Ginny, well, she lay down between the two front seats with her feet under the dashboard, her head back toward me. We pulled out. The VC opened fire on us. Quickly, quietly I said to the Lord, "If it's now, it's okay!"

The sergeant shoved it in reverse, and we shot back around the guardhouse. He pulled out again. The VC opened up on us the second time. They had to be shooting around us on purpose. They couldn't have missed. They were just a few yards away. We were now stopped at the entrance as they continued firing. We couldn't move. Shells were flying back and forth in front of us. An Armored Personnel Carrier (APC) to our right at the end of the road was firing on a VC tank to our left at the other end of the road. Ginny looked at me. Our eyes met, not a word was spoken. We knew!

Then a lull! The shelling stopped!

The sergeant pulled out to the right, his foot to the floor, putting Mario Andretti to shame. Dr. Varano stood up shouting at the APC, "Don't shoot! Don't shoot!" making himself a better target.

Past the APC we flew, hung a left, then two blocks, a quick left then right into our driveway. I finally looked up from the floor boards and saw that the sergeant and I were the only ones still in the jeep. I wanted to thank him, but I couldn't talk. I walked into the living room. Sheila heard us come in and came out of the bedroom.

Dr. Dickstein looked at me. "I've never been shot at like that before!"

"Yeah," was all that was left in me to reply.

"What did you go for!" Sheila shot back. And with that I went to the kitchen to drink a couple gallons of water.

Dr. Varano yelled through our window. "Pack a bag, you're coming to MACV."

I wanted to get out of that house as fast as I could, but Sheila didn't want to leave. I asked Dr. Varano to come in and talk to her.

I was packed. Ginny was still packing. I told her I was going over. More soldiers had pulled up out front, anxious to get us there.

As we pulled into MACV, I thought how different it looked now than it did seven months earlier. Rather than the quaint French villa it had been, now it took on the look of a military compound on alert, which it was. Gone was the grass, just dirt now. Sandbags pressed against the barbed fence. Coils of barbed wire lined the road in front, blocking any traffic from the other direction.

I went into the mess hall, got a cup of coffee out of gallons, in what looked like a washtub. I took it to a bench on the back porch of the villa. Then a soldier sat next to me. He took my rifle and looked at it closely, making sure a round wasn't in the chamber, and began to tell me all about it.

Then I saw Ginny and Sheila coming toward me down the porch. Ginny took Sheila into the briefing room and put her on the sofa.

We heard the deafening sound of rocket fire overhead. Ginny and I ran up the stairs to the second-floor porch that jetted out of the villa. Dr. Dickstein and Dr. Varano and several others were already there. Gunships were putting in air strikes all over town under Colonel Girdner's direction from a chopper.

I had my camera with me and started shooting pictures of the gunships the instant I heard the rocket fired.

After I had taken all the pictures I wanted, I looked in on Sheila. I couldn't tell if she was asleep or not since she had her back toward me. I walked out near the gate, leaning against the front end of a jeep. As the air war continued overhead, I looked down at the dirt and thanked God for life.

My mind cleared. The Ellisons!

I yelled up to the second-floor porch.

"Someone has to go get the Ellisons!"

Dr. Dickstein came down, found a driver and a jeep, and took off to get them. I wanted to go, but he wouldn't let me.

I leaned back against a jeep, waiting!

The army doctor was visiting Phu Vinh. He liked being here and considered it R&R, until today. Leaning up against the jeep next to me, he said, "I hope this doesn't last too long. I've only brought five changes of underwear!"

Phu Vinh was being chewed up by rocket fire, bit by bit, block by block.[1] What was the most concern? Was it life? No! Underwear! War humor had no equal!

Where are the Ellisons? Where were they? Then I just knew they wouldn't be coming. They would stay where they were, and they would be alright.

Dr. Dickstein returned without them. They would stay home.

I returned to the porch and watched the air strikes the rest of the afternoon.

Colonel Girdner returned to MACV just before dark. Everyone was called into the briefing room:

"Several hundred VC came into town this morning. They were in the hospital, high school, lumber yard, theater, and pagodas. They had stored a cache of weapons three weeks prior in the pagodas. We believe we have eliminated most of their leadership. I want a 100 percent alert at 3 a.m."

---

[1] 350 VC from the north and 350 VC from the south invaded Phu Vihn January 31, 1968.

That night the province chief and his family slept in the briefing room. We were given an office with three cots, a desk, and dresser and were glad to have it. We washed up, and I put clean fatigues back on.

Just before we went to sleep, I thought of a really funny joke. I knew this would get a laugh: "If this is how they are going to celebrate TET, I don't want to be here next year!"

Neither Sheila nor Ginny laughed to my disappointment. I'd have to come up with something funnier than that; but how?

I slept well until 3 a.m. I grabbed my rifle and a helmet that was on the desk and walked down to the back porch to where I saw a soldier. "What are you doing here?" he said.

It seemed I heard that question once before!

"There's 100 percent alert now," I replied.

"Well, we didn't mean you!"

I turned, went back to bed, feeling a bit rejected.

Early in the morning Colonel Girdner knocked and came into our room. "The way things look right now, we think most of the VC slipped out of town during the night. One good thing about all this is the power lines are out and Can Tho doesn't know about us. That means Phu Vinh isn't on the news back home. I think you can go to the hospital, but I'm sending an escort with you. I want you to go together and come back together."

After we helped with triage, Ginny and I went to our wards and Sheila scrubbed in surgery.

As I walked across the courtyard, I saw the high school across the street, full of holes with part of a wall gone, but it still stood. The wall around the hospital wasn't as protective looking now with more gaping holes and a shorter height. And then there was the supply building, blown up into rubble by the VC, and on top of the heap of unrecognizable medical supplies lay green plastic gallon jugs that once housed Phisohex. A burned-out jeep stood next to it all.

Co Thu was already on the ward when I got there. After finding out her family was well, I asked about Kim Hoa, an interpreter I knew well.

Co Thu replied, "She is here somewhere. Early yesterday she came to the hospital because she knew the Americans would be here. On the street out front she saw wounded ARVN soldiers trying to get in the hospital so she stopped and helped pull them off the road and got them into the operating room. But when she saw no one was here, she ran back to her family."

I thought, Kim Hoa, you really are something! You could have been killed for your trust in us.

I set up a dressing cart and started wound care for a long day ahead.

The power was out. There was enough sterile equipment to start some surgery. The back-up generator needed some repair, and several men from MACV were working on it.

Back at MACV that evening, the mess hall was abuzz with talk of yesterday's events. A pregnant lady couldn't get to the maternity ward but was able to make it to the recovery room. Dr. McDougal went to help her, and a few minutes later came out holding a new life. Then Dr. McDougal was operating on a little girl when the CIA agent came in and told him to leave.

He turned the surgery over to Dr. Huong. Dr. McDougal had to leave, but he didn't like it.

At the briefing that evening, Colonel Girdner said most all of South Vietnam[2] is under attack.

That meant it was big news back home. That meant my parents would know. If only I could let them know I was all right!

We were all exhausted. I slept soundly.

Before going to the hospital Friday morning, I put the rifle under the dresser at MACV. No one could see it there. I couldn't leave it at the house for the VC to possibly take.

I was in the middle of wound care when a medic came in. "They want you in the OR. They're having a meeting."

Everyone was there. The CIA agent then spoke, and it went something like this. "The colonel is spending too much time wor-

---

[2] Out of 44 provinces, 36 were under attack.

rying about you three. He expects another attack, and he wants you evacuated to Can Tho."

My heart sank! I desperately did not want to go. I just wanted to stay where people cared about me and whom I cared about. Another attack! So what! I didn't care what happened. If I could just stay here!

I asked to stop by the Ellisons for a minute before we left to tell them where we were going and to see that they were all right.

The chopper was waiting for us on the far side of the hospital in the "baseball field." We had played one game there.

In Can Tho we were met at the airport by men in full combat gear, then rushed through deserted streets of sandbags and barbed wire to the apartment building where the nurses were quartered. Sheila stayed with a nurse friend from Washington. Ginny stayed with another nurse, and I stayed with Betty Stahl.

"We haven't been to the hospital since Tuesday," she said. "The doctors and some Vietnamese medical staff have been working every day, but there was such sniper fire they wouldn't let us go. We are all going in the morning."

Dear Lord, give me strength, I thought.

I hadn't brought uniforms in my naivete that I wouldn't be working. Lynn Kelly solved that problem with scrub gowns. A burlap sack with arm holes is like a scrub gown, but with more style.

Saturday morning came too soon. We all climbed into vehicles and were escorted to the hospital.

Ginny went off with a nurse to her ward. I was dropped off at the women's surgical ward.

A huge square room where beds lined the walls all around, pushed together so patients could lie crosswise, accommodating more. The overflow covered the floor. There was no time for triage. I quickly glanced around the ward, looking for the most critical. They all were critical after days of dehydration, heat, and a kaleidoscope of wounds.

At my feet was a woman in shock who needed an IV started. I ran to the pharmacy, picked up IVs, morphine, and syringes, then over to central service and set up a dressing cart.

I found some help to take five patients to the OR. That cleared the floor some, so I could move around.

Every patient roundabout that did not have a head wound got morphine, then I started wound care, removing shrapnel and cleaning and dressing burns.

Soon I needed more supplies, and heading to central service, I could see into the large open emergency room. A boy lay as a skeleton on a litter[3], dead, with his arms raised to heaven as if begging for help. A woman lay close by, dying in slow silent agony with every labored breath.

Sunday was the same. Again, I worked alone on the ward.

That evening I saw Lynn and asked her, "Isn't there a nurse assigned to women's surgical?"

"Yes, there is!" she shot back angrily.

Monday morning came with an abundance of help. The nurse assigned to the ward was there working, as was an International Voluntary in Service (IVS) man. I was teaching him wound care. Then another nurse came, and Lynn was there doing wound care also. Then she said, "I want to see the three of you over at my apartment at lunch."

I was so excited. We're going back to Phu Vinh! I knew we wouldn't be here long.

We were standing in her living room waiting for the good news.

"You can't go back to Phu Vinh. They need volunteers to go to My Tho. I don't know the security."

Hum, I thought. I don't know about volunteering, hum.

Ginny said, "I'll go!"

I said, "I'll go!"

Sheila said, "I'll go!"

---

[3] *A litter is used to bring in wounded from the field.*

CHAPTER 9

My Tho

We were met at Can Tho airport by two AID men looking to see what bridges were still standing. After flying around parts of the Delta, the plane then banked over My Tho. Looking down I saw roads outlining rectangles filled with hills and mounds of rubble where life had once been. I was reminded of pictures I'd seen of Hiroshima. I soon would learn that one-third of My Tho had been destroyed.

The airport was a dirt strip with a building the size of a hotdog stand. Gunfire echoed in the distance. Did anyone know we were coming? Inside an air force captain was writing in his ledger, "Do you see those trees over there? Look to the right of the tall one. See it? The VC flag tied there? It's a booby trap. They know we like souvenirs."

He turned back to his writing. I asked if anyone would be coming to pick us up.

"Soon," he mumbled.

Not soon enough two jeeps pulled up with heavily armed soldiers. The streets looked familiar, sandbags and barbed wire everywhere.

We pulled up in front of the nurses' house across the street from the hospital. It was still the lunch hour, and they were all there. We knew each other from Washington, and Edith had been my roommate for a short time before being sent over to Vietnam early.

This day, Monday morning, was the first day they had been to the hospital since the start of the TET offensive six days ago. The nurses' deep sadness and despair was palpable in that house riddled with shrapnel.

They had found 1,500 wounded patients, 600 were crammed inside the hospital and 900 lay outside around the grounds, everywhere. Some had died in place, waiting!

The hospital was two stories high. At both ends of a large open corridor were wide steel stairs, as you would see in a factory, leading up to two separate floors. A gaping hole in the center of the roof pointed to where a mortar round made its way in.

But the hospital and its out buildings were not what first grabbed my attention. The multitudes of wounded covering walkways and the courtyard with families scurrying in and out of the culverts under the hospital caring for their loved ones in filth held me spellbound.

I moved along, keeping up with Edith, who took me to central service where I was given an emesis basin, 4 x 4s, normal saline, and a hemostat. What am I supposed to do with that? I thought. If it wasn't so tragic, it'd be funny.

Oh, God, please get me through this day!

The electricity had been out, which meant no autoclave or sterile equipment, so an antiseptic solution was used, and surgery continued.

At the hospital an American civilian surgeon headed up the medical team. But desperately was more help needed, so four medics and Major Mosley and Colonel Blackwell, a surgeon, were sent in from Dong Tham Evac. Center.

That evening the three of us were taken to the civilian doctor's house where a major was also staying. C rations were dinner, as had been lunch at the nurses' house. We were then led to the second floor where mattresses, with blankets and pillows, covered the floor. Finally sleep!

A new day filled with hope!

Ginny and I triaged patients, then I worked with Dr. Mosley giving penicillin shots and doing wound care.

On my way over to the nurses' house for lunch, I passed a room where I heard Colonel Blackwell talking to the medics and others. I went in.

"I want two nurses to work all night," he said.

"I will, and I think I can get someone else," I responded quickly.

I ran to the nurses' house, I was so happy. We're going to get this place cleaned up! We have leadership! The nurses were all there. I was looking at Ginny when I said, "Colonel Blackwell wants two nurses to work all night and I'm going to."

Ginny said she would.

I looked around the room. What I had seen on their faces when I first arrived was still there—sadness and despair in spite of all the added help, and I think I knew why. I felt it in the short time I'd been here. No one truly cared for them. Their house was turned into a collection of shrapnel, and they, since TET, had been living in a dormitory at the Navy Compound. In Phu Vinh we all cared for each other. I didn't see that here.

When we finished work at 5:00, we were taken back to the civilian doctor's house for a dinner of C rations. Ginny and I were picked up at 7:00 and brought back to the hospital with Colonel Blackwell and the medics. We gave more penicillin shots and triaged.

The Filipino surgical team was also there working. This was the first time I'd met them. At the start of TET, they had just made it out alive to a bunker before their house was destroyed. They lost everything. And they also were staying at the Navy Compound.

At 1:00 a.m. we took a break over to the nurses' house. We talked for a while, then Colonel Blackwell said, "This is enough for one day!" We were taken back to the doctor's house.

I fell onto the mattress in my filthy clothes, exhausted! Incoming! A heavy barrage! The major yelled to us to come down under the stairs. I took my blanket and we sat. All I wanted was sleep. I put my blanket out onto the floor, lay down, and was instantly out cold.

A round hit close! I bolted straight up with a loud yell coming out of my mouth. Ginny said, "It's all right! It's all right!"

The next morning, we bid adieu to the doctor's house and were moved into the Navy Compound.

A lieutenant had given up his quarters for us. A tiny office in the front, just large enough for a desk and filing cabinet, and back of that, a room with three cots and a bathroom to the side.

The compound was quite large, compared to MACV at Phu Vinh. The main building, towering over all of it, was called appropriately at the time the "Victory Hotel." And in the back of that was a string of small buildings conjoined, and at one end the dormitory. Our room was conveniently located across from the eight steps leading to the first floor of the "hotel" and right into the navy mess hall. And can they ever cook! My taste buds woke from months of slumber into ecstasy!

After settling in we walked the three blocks to the hospital. Not being allowed to walk anywhere in Phu Vinh, it now never occurred to me how unsafe this could be.

Surgery was in full swing everywhere—in the four ORs, a side room, and even outside on the walkway. The OR was for head, chest, and abdominal wounds.

Many amputations needed to be done before gangrene took their lives. Standing over a patient lying on an elevated bench was Colonel Blackwell and Edith in cap and gown just beginning to cut through the bone of the man's leg. An oil drum nearby was almost filled to capacity with amputations. Not far, a child was playing with a limb.

Everyone settled into a job; Sheila to the OR, Ginny to the first floor, and I went up to the left half of the second floor. With a dressing cart I debrided burns, removed shrapnel that I could reach with a hemostat that wasn't near an artery nor in a bone.

Finally, I reached the old man in the far corner of the room, his wife with him. I could see kindness in their eyes as they greeted me. I unwrapped the old dressing on his left thigh. The wound was six inches long and to the bone, full of purulent drainage with two screws holding the femur together. After cleaning, I noticed the soft tissue was healthy looking and seemed to have good circulation. He had had surgery, probably before TET.

The next day his wound was again filled with "pus." At the same time, a little girl had a large piece of shrapnel sticking out of her sternum. Miraculously she had survived. Down on the first floor I found an American Army doctor I hadn't seen before. He came and removed the shrapnel. I so much wanted him to look at the man's leg and tell me what more I can do for him—like, how much penicillin could I give him to be effective while I was at work?

But I knew he was overwhelmed downstairs. I didn't dare ask for more of his time. This decision I would regret for the rest of my life.

"Who is supposed to be working up here?" I asked.

"The civilian doctor!"

"Where will I find him?"

"You'll probably find him in the casting room," he replied with a hint of anger in his voice.

From now on I was to make one bad decision after another!

I went to the casting room. He was there. I told him about the man and described the condition of his leg. I asked him to come up and see him. I wanted him to start working on his ward!

"Bring him down here," he said.

Oh, why didn't I walk away and find the army doctor?

But I found a couple of ARVN troops, and they brought the man to the hall outside the casting room.

The doctor was gone! I asked the Vietnamese women working there where he had gone. They didn't know. I told them the doctor was to look at the man's leg, and I left to get back to work. I expected him to come and talk to me about the old man. He didn't! So later I went looking for the doctor and my patient. The doctor wasn't there, but the old man was on a table in the casting room in a full-body cast extending down his left leg to the ankle. It would have been comical if it hadn't been such a horrible experience for him. I told them to take the cast off, and at the same time the doctor showed up. I again told him about the man and his leg and asked would he please get back to me after he'd seen the leg and have the patient brought up to his ward.

There comes a time when common sense supersedes trust in someone, but I hadn't reached that point with medical personnel yet.

The afternoon dragged on. No word, no patient came. I was not leaving work until I found the old man! I went down to the first floor again, but this time I headed for the enormous ward filled with suffering humanity. How could I ever find him here? I passed down the hallway lined with the operating rooms, each opening into the hallway. One door was open. I looked in. This wonderful, kind old man was on the table with his left leg amputated at the hip. The civilian doctor was standing there with others.

I turned and walked to the bottom of the stairs. Starting up a few steps, I sat, numb, staring into space.

Before the week was out, we had all been vaccinated against cholera, typhoid, and, of all things, the plague.

My work was divided between wound care, typhoid vaccinations, tetanus antitoxin, and ongoing penicillin shots.

And the wounded? They just kept coming!

Colonel Blackwell, Major Mosley, and the medics had to get back to Dong Tham Evac. Center. I felt a great loss. Their help, leadership, and encouragement was gone.

The Navy Compound held a church service Sunday and then we were taken on a drive around My Tho and shown the destruction. Burned-out buildings and buses, then everywhere heaps and heaps of waste where life and community once stood. There was nothing new here! Always the same since the beginning of time.

Our driver then told us that North Korea had captured one of our ships called the *Pueblo*, and all the crew had been taken prisoner. He said it happened a few days before TET. Now there were more people to pray for, I thought.

It didn't take us long to "wise up" and abandon the nurses' house and its contents of C rations. We were glad to walk back to the Navy Compound for lunch.

One day in the mess hall an officer told me that an AID nurse had been killed in Vinh Long Province. "If things get really bad here, we will probably take you out on a PBR boat," he added.

A PBR boat? What's that?

Ginny said she needed help downstairs. The first floor was as packed now as it had ever been since we arrived; and why wouldn't it be, the patients just kept moving in from outside.

We both were working in a small corner using the same dressing cart; Ginny cleaning wounds from a lady on one cot and I debriding burns from a lady on another cot who was cradling a two-week-old baby tightly in her arms. The mother was burned down both legs to her toes, and the baby's scalp was burned. The skin on her toes was dead, and Ginny had to help me remove it all—like removing a glove. I thought I was going to be sick.

The burned patient suffers the most, and I was swept along into their agony while caring for them.

Sheila told us she was going out on Leave. She went back to Phu Vinh to get her clothes and pick up our mail, then back to My Tho for the drop-off, and then Leave.

Mail! Finally! I would now know that my parents had heard I was safe! Not so! They hadn't received any of my letters that I had written since TET. It was all I could think about. I was desperate! I prayed for my letters to get to them.

The president's wife, Madame Thieu, came to the hospital with reporters and photographers one afternoon, shook my hand, then said, "Thank you for the good work."

I didn't want my parents back home to see My Tho hospital on the evening news! I never had told them about the patient care nor the conditions here.

Ginny had some things to catch up on back at the compound, so I was walking alone to the hospital early one morning when all of a sudden the Vietnamese started running in the opposite direction. I wanted to run behind a building until I could find out what was happening, but I couldn't because in front of every building was a high cement wall dotted on top with broken glass. I was in a tunnel. I prayed for safety and kept walking toward the hospital entrance.

Just inside I was told to get in the jeep and was taken to headquarters for a briefing.

Reconnaissance had seen VC bringing up heavy artillery around My Tho during the night. We were to get to the Navy Compound and stay there. Another lost day at work! That night had just the usual incoming mortar but no major attack. We must have persuaded the VC to "leave town."

Then Lynn Kelly came for a visit to check on all of us and occupied the empty cot in our bedroom overnight.

Ginny handed me a pamphlet. "Do you believe in angels, Nancy?"

"Yea, I think I do."

"Well, read this. It has a lot to say about them."

I laid it on my cot and went outside.

I saw a Vietnamese man squatting, shaking, crying, and in his arms his little girl of about seven. I went to them and as I came closer I knew the girl was dead. I put my hand on her forehead and saw in the father's face his broken heart.

A corpsman stood watching in the door to "sick bay."

I turned and saw the AID man that had brought them here. Here! And only here, where I was able to escape death for a time. Here! Where he has shattered my peace. I didn't say a word, just turned and walked back into the bedroom and lay on my cot until I knew they had to be gone. I picked up the pamphlet and read: "For He shall give His angels charge over thee, to keep thee in all thy ways."[4]

Ginny and I went to a Bible study that was taught by the lieutenant whose quarters we now occupied. He knew the Word well, and that evening was a blessing to me on this yo-yo ride through My Tho.

In an impromptu moment on a Saturday evening, we all gathered around the mess hall steps; some had guitars and we started singing. Such a happy time it was. It went on for hours until the "boss" came out and told us to go to bed.

Sunday morning the chaplain was unable to come to the Navy Compound, so the lieutenant gave the message. There seemed to always be a remnant of Christians no matter where I went. I was grateful!

That evening around 9:30, I was on the cot ready to go to sleep. Ginny was in the office at the lieutenant's desk reading. Then incoming mortar came, many and close. Out went the light at the desk.

---

[4] Psalm 91:11.

Ginny came into the bedroom propelled by fear, landing under her cot with more grace than a ballerina.

"Get under that cot!" she yelled up.

"I'm not getting on a PBR boat in a nightie," I shot back as I continued to rummage through the suitcase for my clothes in the dark.

I knew they were coming through that door any minute and taking us out of here on a PBR boat, down some river to the South China Sea, up the Co Chien River to anchor out from Vinh Binh Province. A chopper would then come in from somewhere and land on the boat and take us in to Phu Vinh. And if the boat is too small for the chopper? I'd swim it! I'm going back to Phu Vinh.

I finally found the fatigues I had brought for such an occasion.

A round then exploded close, sending shrapnel shooting into the back wall of the bedroom becoming one with it.

That did it! I dove under the cot, landing on the ironing board with the legs side up and that hurt! I shoved it out into the middle of the room, then reached up and grabbed my pillow. No PBR boat!

Gnawing at me was the overwhelming need for the mail. Is this what it's like for a POW? Not knowing if their loved ones know if they are alive or not.

I asked Ginny to come with me to Colonel Schowalter's[5] headquarters.

It was late in the afternoon when he arrived, looking much thinner than I remember from Phu Vinh. He walked with a cane; a cast on his left wrist and from his left ear down his neck staples held together a fresh incision.

He seemed glad to see "his girls," as he affectionately called us.

I told him of our need to know that our families knew we were safe and would very much like to get back to Phu Vinh for the mail. He understood immediately and said we could take his chopper when he was finished for the day tomorrow.

---

[5] Colonel Schowalter had his jugular vein cut by a bullet during the offensive. Soon after medical care he was directing the defense of My Tho. He was decorated for this later. He is also a Medal of Honor recipient from combat in Korea.

We jumped on the chopper. Home again! On the road from the runway to MACV, I asked to run by the Ellisons for just a minute. I needed news.

The sergeant driving looked over at us. "They aren't here. Six of their missionaries were killed at Ban Me Thuot by the North Vietnamese Army (NVA), and three were taken captive.[6] All the wives with small children have been evacuated to Bangkok, and Paul Ellison is out working in another district presently."

We hurried on to MACV and the mail.

"I didn't know where to send it," the corporal said as he handed us this precious sack.

"Keep it here or it will be lost," I replied.

I asked the sergeant to run by the hospital so I could let them know where we were. Then to our house to pick up clothes for leave. Scrub gowns and flip-flops just wouldn't do. Quickly I threw clothes in a bag.

I heard Ginny rummaging through the desk in the dining room. She yelled to me, "What drawer are the leave forms in?"

"I don't know," I replied.

Quiet, calm Ginny was getting out of My Tho on Leave. I had to laugh.

We sped back to the airport with dust flying, but it wasn't soon enough for the crew of the chopper.

How beautiful the Delta was from the air. Rivers small and large weave around shades of green rice paddies with dots of villages. No death from up here.

I rifled through the sack and pulled out a box with six apples—four were rotted, two were eatable. Ginny and I consumed them with joy. What an expense my parents took on to send these apples at my request. Never again would I ask for anything perishable.

---

[6] Hank Blood, a Wycliffe Bible translator working on the Muong translation; Betty Olsen, a missionary nurse, and Mike Benge, a USAID worker were taken captive by the NVA during the TET offensive at Ban Me Thuot. Mike was the only survivor.

I sat on the steps to the mess hall enthralled in the letters. My parents now knew I was safe. Peace at last! Thank you, Lord. I was grateful for Colonel Schowalter who understood.

As I was walking through the Navy Compound one day, I heard behind me a loud shout, "One of my nurses!"

I turned around and there stood Colonel Blackwell in a Class A uniform. I didn't know there was a Class A in Vietnam.

"I'll buy you a cup of coffee," he said.

"What are you doing back here?"

"We came back to give the civilian doctor a medal."

"Oh?" I said.

Colonel Blackwell picked right up on my one-syllable word with the reply, "Well, it's PR."

It was February 28, my dad's birthday and exactly four weeks since the start of the TET offensive. Ginny and I were standing next to the canal in My Tho waiting for a chopper to come in and take us to Saigon.

Beyond the bridge, over the canal, I could see the roof of the hospital. The courtyard and walkways now only held families cooking meals and resting there. The number of patients could now be contained in the building. I turned, watching for the chopper, and never looked back.

CHAPTER 10

Return to Phu Vinh

We rode through the streets of much destruction. Who would have thought Saigon would be hit like this. Soon I found out Phu Vinh was still closed to us. I hurried over to Max's office, in a much too small room for the huge desk he sat behind. He held absolute power over arranging Leave.

"I'm going on Leave to Bangkok, Penang, and Singapore," I spoke with confidence.

"What Leave?" he shot back.

"I was here January 12 and made out Leave forms," I replied, sinking into despair!

"Well, let me go check," he said, leaving the room.

My mind racing—Lord, I don't want to tell you what I can and can't do, but I can't go back to My Tho. Please, Lord, I can't go back, I can't, I can't...!

"You're all set," Max said, coming through the door. "You can pick your tickets up tomorrow."

As I left his office, I thought God does make a way of escape, that we are able to bear it.

Ginny and I stayed at the hostel for AID personnel that evening.

"Do you know where Israel got its name?" Ginny asked.

"No, where?" I replied.

Ginny went on to tell me the story of Jacob wrestling all night with God: "And He said, 'Thy name shall be called no more Jacob, but Israel'" (Genesis 32:28).

I turned over in bed to go to sleep. My thoughts went back to when I prayed for God to "make the war better." James 4:3 reads, "Ye ask, and receive not, because ye ask amiss—."

How I then tried to "fix it," wrestling with God by fasting, while all this time God was at work keeping me safe until I would realize I was to pray, not for the war, but for each life preserved as in Genesis 32:30.

March 2 we both left Tan Son Nhut airport on Leave. Ginny was on her way to Hong Kong for a week.

As the plane lifted off, a sense of freedom, joy, peace, all in one, came over me as when I left for Nepal, but now more intense. I'd be seeing Eunice and Linda soon in Bangkok. What a treat!

I called the Alliance Hostel from the hotel. I was told they had left and gone up-country to see Paul's brother and his family, who were also missionaries. A disappointment for me!

I then placed a call home. Dad ran upstairs to get on the extension. I wanted to cry out, "They tried to kill me," but my parents must not ever know this, so I talked about something meaningless like which way was this call going, east to west? Oh, how good to hear their voices.

So much to see in Bangkok; riding on a market boat down the river, which would stop for people to shop; Thai dancing at the hotel and to a game farm with other tourists.

Then on to Penang, an island twenty-eight miles in diameter off the west coast of the Malaysian peninsula.

The Lone Pine Lodge with surrounding cabins sat on bleached white sand overlooking the bay as the sun danced across the clearest blue water I'd even seen.

In a flash I was in my bathing suit with my Bible heading down the beach to perch on one of the boulders jetting out into the water. A Malaysian young man came with his fishing pole, standing high up on a boulder closer to land. After not catching anything for a time, he quit and came down across in front of me and dove in. Then he popped up, reaching out to me with a shell in his hand to admire. Such fun! Then I dove in and we both swam for a time, chasing after a jellyfish fruitlessly, then popping up to show each other the new-found treasure in our hand in silence. Then he jumped out, picked up his fishing pole, and was gone—the interlude over.

The next day in the lodge office, as the rain plummeted onto the metal roof making it hard to hear, I was able to call home again! This time the conversation was more relaxed and flowed in love.

It was Sunday so I walked off looking to find a church in English, which I did. I noticed that all the houses were elevated on stilts. I thought this was so, probably, to keep out predators and high water.

The next two days were beautiful and wonderfully repetitious of when I first arrived—swimming and relaxing.

A couple I'd met on the plane to Bangkok were at the lodge. They had decided to cancel their plans and stay in Penang.

Nevertheless, I had decided to go on to Singapore. It rained most of the time, so I found myself in jewelry stores buying gifts for my nieces, nephews, Mom and Dad, and myself, spending lots of money and enjoying it.

The huge hotel I stayed in wrapped itself around a large swimming pool that always looked abandoned. I stood on the diving board for some time thinking how good it was to be alive!

March 16, Saturday, I arrived back in Saigon. Was it possible Tan Son Nhut airport could be more chaotic than usual? We lined up for customs, staying riveted to the same spot for what seemed like an eternity; then being rushed, people fighting over my suitcase as to who would win to carry it to the vehicle for a tip. Funny, it hadn't bothered me so much before.

I was the only passenger in the van as it pulled out. A block later the driver stopped, an American civilian leaped in, out of breath and very on edge. We were both going to the AID (CORDS) office. He wanted to talk, and I just happened to be there. He said he worked in the health department, then asked what I did. I told him about Phu Vinh and that I was an AID nurse and had just gotten back from leave to Bangkok and Pen…, when he interrupted.

"Do you know the State Department is now paying the nurses coming here ten thousand dollars a year? It's just the guilt State has, you know, bringing you nurses over here to win the hearts and minds of the Vietnamese people—that's a laugh!"

"But we do help—," I started to say.

He continued, his anger unabated. "State doesn't want to open any more stations for AID nurses. The nurses now training in Hawaii want to come over, so State is asking if any nurses here would like to go home, completing their tour in twelve months instead of eighteen."

It was right then I decided I'd be going home in June, not December!

We pulled up in front of CORDS. I checked in at the office and was told Phu Vinh was now open. I could go back anytime. That was the best news I had since I left so long ago it seemed.

It being Saturday, I knew Dede Aaron would be home. She was always glad to have company, even if unexpected—she's a rare type that way.

We knew each other from Washington. She had a sofa I would sack out on from time to time, but was careful not to wear out my welcome. Dede worked as a secretary for AID. She had a car, knew the best restaurants, had parties on her roof, and she was fun and funny to be around. I felt like conversation so I went over.

The next morning Dede and I were sitting in the International Church waiting for the service to start. I looked to my left and at the end of the pew, I saw standing, Paul, Eunice, and Linda. They moved in next to me. I can't describe the joy I felt. By far the best moment in Vietnam.

Talking outside after church, Paul had come up to Saigon to meet them coming in from Bangkok. They would be returning to Phu Vinh on Wednesday, and I was returning tomorrow.

Ginny and Sheila were still at the hospital when I got in.

There was great comfort to be back in a place with trusted friends and familiarity that can be called "home," at least for a time.

That evening I learned the ARVN had a new rocket launcher on the corner. Just then it fired, sending me aloft out of the chair.

I had gone over to MACV to pick up the mail and to retrieve my rifle I had left under the dresser in the room we had stayed in during TET. Pulling it out, I saw the strap was missing, but for the two places where it had been attached, little nubbins were left. I knew immediately what had happened. Those rats ate it for the salt in the sweat. Laughing, I mumbled, "Is there anything they won't eat? I hope they choke on the buckle!"

By morning I was still reading my way through the mail, but I had to put it down and get to the hospital.

From time to time I had shown others the dressing technique, but they had gone to other wards or transferred. Maybe that wasn't so bad. They may have followed through with what they had learned. However, I had more teaching to do.

Tuesdays, I'd clean the ward. The side walls folded together, which opened the ward to the walkways, allowing the beds to be pulled out so I could mop the floor. Then I'd wash the stationary walls on both ends of the ward. The mothers and I would get laughing and that would increase our friendship.

Two Buddhist nuns came into the ward. They were watching me at wound care. I began showing them the dressing technique. They were interested; they learned well. That was what I wanted to do for a long time.

After TET no longer did we line up at the hospital in the morning while the Vietnamese National Anthem played and the flag raised. That was over!

Soon the VC were at it again with mortar attacks. However, this time they chose midweek along with weekends. The TET offensive had, after all, started on a Wednesday, so the theory of just weekend attacks didn't hold up any longer.

I was tired of my sleep being interrupted with "incoming." So I tried not to react, and it worked. I'd wake up when the mortar started, but I'd stay in bed and I usually went back to sleep.

A few days after I got back to Phu Vinh, Lynn Kelly called. She affirmed the Tour of Duty had been lowered from eighteen months to twelve. I told her I wanted to go home in June.

March 30, Saturday at twelve noon, I was standing next to a stretcher in the OR waiting for Ginny to come so we could leave for the weekend. Sheila was in central service washing her hands.

In came a man toward me, shaking so badly he could hardly stand, holding a baby covered in blood. He thrust the baby into my arms and left. I held him at a distance, looking for injuries, his feet pushing up and down against the stretcher, his arms flailing rapidly, eyes focused, screaming. I quickly looked him over and found a small cut on his forehead. Where did all this blood come from? I pulled him tight to me so I could make a steri-strip to close the cut. Ginny had come in and got saline and washed his forehead.

Then two men came with a man on the litter with one leg hanging by some flesh. I ran with the baby out of the OR, down four steps, across the yard, up four steps and deposited the baby into the arms of the first mother I saw on my ward. I ran back to the OR so fast it seemed like flight. There was a woman lying on a litter in shock. I knelt down to start the IV that was already hung. I needed something more. I got up, running to central service, when I heard a scream so piercing I stopped and turned to the sound coming out of a little girl of about ten, both legs blown off at the knee, both tibias intact with bone marrow running onto the stretcher. Then she raised her thighs. The scream got worse as she saw what was left of her. I wanted to put myself over her so she couldn't see, but I couldn't move. I wanted President Johnson right here, right now, and I was going to ask him, "Is anything worth this?" A Vietnamese OR tech came running with two tourniquets. They pushed her across in front of me into the operating room and the screaming stopped. She died!

I don't remember anything after that.[7] I don't know if I stood there for four and a half hours, if someone sat me down or if I worked. The next thing I knew it was 5:00 and I was standing just inside the recovery room. Sheila came and was standing next to me. I was looking down at a woman whose face was all wrapped. Both arms were gone above the elbow; both legs were gone above the knee. Around the bed Dr. Varano was caring for her with others.

I turned, walked through the recovery room, out the door at the end, out the screen door of the OR and to the vehicle. Ginny and Sheila came right along.

A Lambretta,[8] carrying a dozen or more people, had driven over a land mine. This was my worst day in Vietnam and a lot of other people's worst day, not the least of which were the Vietnamese.

The next day after church we had coffee at the Ellisons. I told them I was leaving in June. Paul asked why.

"We shouldn't be here," I responded. "Not you, well, that's different. I mean us. When we're here, the war just gets bigger and bigger, with no end in sight. Nothing gets better."

I stopped there because I knew they liked being here. But after TET, I thought we were going nowhere. And a lost war wasn't the hardest for me to contemplate. But oh, all the deaths and hurt people in families back home and here. How could the president admit we'd made a mistake, we misevaluated, we misunderstood, and we misinterpreted this war!

In the afternoon we went over to the orphanage with the medics and Dr. Dickstein to care for the children. I needed this.

We heard later the president would not run for reelection. Good, I thought! Anything's got to be better than this—or would it!

---

[7] This is dissociative amnesia. Ginny told me years later, when I asked what I had done for the rest of the four hours of that day, that I had worked.
[8] Lambretta is a motor scooter or a motorcycle with a cart attached.

CHAPTER 11

Mini TET

Back on pediatrics I was told a two-year-old boy and his mother had been on the Lambretta that drove over the mine. He was not hurt. I picked him up and carried him to the women's surgical ward to look for his mother.

One of the patients recognized him. Through tears she told Ginny and I that his mother had been killed and that her child had been killed.

The boy clung to me and I to him as we started back to the children's ward. I thought, children without their mothers, mothers without their children. I wanted to sit down on the walkway and cry, cry without end! Ginny walked with me!

A few days later, April 5, we heard Dr. King had been shot and killed. My first thoughts were for our African-American friends over at MACV. I knew of unrest back home, however, but not until I returned did I see so much violence fueled by great hate and anger.

The doctors were at the house after church. An officer rushed in. One of his soldiers had been hit bad. "He's way out, isolated. They're trying to bring him to the river so the navy can pick him up. A chopper is waiting to take you to the LST."

Before he had finished talking, Dr. Leonard was on his feet and out the door.

When Dr. Leonard returned, he stayed in the pre-fab for a time. Dr. Varano was with him. Sometime later they both came in. He then was able to tell us what happened.

"They had an awful time getting him to the river. He'd lost a lot of blood when I saw him on the LST. In the chopper I started plasma. He seemed to stabilize a little, but I was worried by the time we got him to Dong Tham Evac. Center. When he came through their door, six people went to work on him, each doing a different job. One pumped blood into the jugular, another cut his clothes off, then under X-ray and into the OR. It was something to see a team work with such precision."

He hesitated, not wanting to speak what we already knew. "He had just lost too much blood. He didn't make it."

A medic, Sergeant Powell, was having a birthday. Another excuse for a party. Most of MACV was coming and bringing a sawed-off, sliced-up oil drum to hold the charcoal with enough steaks for the multitude. And in our midst the joy of laughter.

Later that day a pilot stopped by. He said he was piloting the plane that flew over Pau Vinh the morning of January 31.

"When I looked down, I saw VC everywhere. Right then I was called back to Can Tho. I just said goodbye to all of you. I was sure I'd never see any of you again."

Everyone came to the orphanage in the afternoon on Easter Sunday. MACV came with dozens of bright-colored eggs. Vietnamese that I knew from the hospital also came. The children wore new outfits of blue-and-white stripes, their faces all smiles and laughter. I stood watching these happy children unhurt, pain free.

Ginny had thought Linda had been four years old for a very long time.

"Linda, when do you turn five?"

"Her birthday is May 26," Eunice replied.

When I got in the house, I looked on the calendar. "May 26 is Sunday. We can go to her party," I told Ginny.

"Don't you think you should wait to be invited?" Ginny responded.

"OK, I'll invite us the next time I see Eunice." I remembered what Paul had said last Christmas—"that the dollhouse would give Linda a lot of playtime."

That gave me an idea. I wrote home to Mom and Dad to see if they could find a doll that walks and talks. They did. She was perfect. Wind her up and she'd walk, stiff legged, across the living room. Pull the cord in her back and she became vocal with a near endless repertoire of phrases. And she had red hair, like Linda.

Near the end of April, we three and Colonel Girdner were invited to the LST for dinner. The chopper picked us up. We were taken all over the ship, from gun turrets to the control room, ending in the officers' dining room. The men on this ship had been part of keeping us safe for a long time.

May 1 is Labor Day in Vietnam and with it came cellulitis in my right hand quickly mushrooming to my elbow. Dr. Leonard lanced it, and with hot packs and penicillin injections twice a day, that Sheila and Ginny were obliged to give, it healed.

Any infection or any illness, for that matter, in Vietnam was rapidly transformed into great danger and requires immediate attention.

In early May Sheila left Phu Vinh on her way home. Another reason for a party—for her.

At 2:45 a.m. Phu Vinh came under the heaviest mortar attack ever. Worse even than the beginning of the TET offensive on January 31. It was May 5 and this offensive would be known as "mini TET."[9] Ginny and I stayed in Phu Vinh this time. We went to the hospital every day. The casualties weren't overwhelming, as in My Tho. We received word Saigon had been heavily attacked again. Everyone said it was to give the North Vietnamese a better advantage in bargaining power. Who can figure any of this out. All I knew nothing had changed—for the better—since I'd been here that I know of and no one has ever been able to tell me anything different.

---

[9] May 1968 would be the bloodiest month of the war for the Americans. 2,416 Americans died.

The two nurses arrived from Hawaii right in the middle of the offensive. Marsha was assigned to the children's ward and Beverly to the recovery room. They learned fast and said they were glad to be here. I remembered how I felt when I first arrived. I could understand their enthusiasm. A party was held at the house so the doctors and medics could meet them.

During part of their first week we spent time in the OR in triage with many casualties. I prayed for Marsha and Beverly that their time here would go well for them.

Interpreters at the hospital, Ong Duc and Co Ha, were married in a Buddhist ceremony May 20. She wore a white gown. They looked radiant as they stood facing each other in front of the ancestral altar in the bride's living room. A mediator was selected who knew both families and acted as a go-between on their behalf. The matriarch of the bride's family was seated at a table in the middle of the room where the "bride price" had been placed. The mediator told of how they met and something about each family, then displayed the content of the box holding the "bride price." He then asked the matriarch of the groom's family if this sum is acceptable. She would always answer affirmatively since the price had already been agreed upon before the wedding. Then both matriarchs' toast each other's families. The bride and groom would then each light a candle, turn toward the altar, and bow and pay honor to their ancestors. Wine was then given to the couple and both families for a toast to long life and happiness. They were then married.

We all followed to the back part of the house where tables had been set up and on each a menu listing seven courses. The women of both families served the endless supply of delicious food as the couple moved from table to table in happy conversation.

I sometimes think of Ong Duc and Co Ha and of their children they may have had and how their lives had been in the Vietnam of today.

Finally, Linda's birthday party was to be held on Saturday, May 25. I kept the doll safe in my closet and now it would soon be in the arms of the little girl it was meant for. I had wrapped the box so Linda just had to lift off the top at the bow.

I saw Dr. Dickstein that morning. He said, "I'd like to go to Linda's party, but all I have to give her is this," holding up a small metal toy car.

"Anything you'd give her, she'd love it," I replied.

So off we went, Dr. Dickstein with the toy car, Ginny with the doll clothes she'd made, and I with the doll.

From the living room we could see into the dining room with twelve children around a large table. I had never seen Vietnamese children dressed this way before. All the girls had on white dresses, socks, and shoes that shined, and in their hair, a ribbon. The boys wore white shirts, black pants, and instead of sandals they also had socks and shoes. They all started skipping around the table; picking up the rays of the sun across the room, Linda's red curly hair shone brightly.

The doll in the box became the centerpiece in the living room. Eunice brought Linda in. She lifted off the top, looked in, and gave a soft squeal of joy.

Eunice told me when they put Linda to bed, she would tell them, "I can stay up longer, see!" and pull the cord on the doll, finding the phrase to support her claim. From then on Linda and the doll were never far apart. And I received the best gift: to give Linda more playtime and joy.

CHAPTER 12

The Long Way Home

Dr. Leonard was awarded the Bronze Star with Valor for his work during the TET offensive. Under fire he saved the life of a CIA man[10] and others with help.

It was time to go home. Dr. Leonard and I were leaving a day apart. The party was at our house. Colonel Girdner, the province chief, the Milphap team, and the Vietnamese hospital staff—all were there.

Co Thu gave me high heels, with replacement heels no less. The medical team gave me a Vietnamese photo album. I had never realized they were aware of my interest in photography. Then I was presented with a certificate from the province chief for my work at the hospital on January 31.

The next evening, May 27, we were invited to the CIA agents' house for a steak dinner. First, they had to know when we were coming in order to turn off the "juice" in the 15-foot electric fence that engulfed their residence.

The next morning Dr. Leonard left Phu Vinh for home surrounded by an entourage that came to see him off.

That evening Paul and Eunice invited Ginny and me for dinner. Then Linda sat on my lap as I looked through their wedding album. They gave me a vase, which I still cherish.

---

[10] I hesitate to use the name of any CIA agent here.

I got to the Phu Vinh runway early to be sure and not miss the plane home. Colonel Girdner, Dr. Dickstein, Co Thu, Ginny, and the two newly arrived nurses were all there as were Paul, Eunice, and Linda, holding tightly to the doll.

Two choppers then landed. One of the pilots brought me over to them. He asked, "Do you know what a 'fly-bye' is?"

"Never heard of it," I replied.

He continued, "When we take off, we will let out colored flares streaming behind as recognition for your service here."

The choppers lifted off, pouring out ribbons of bright colors as they climbed and were gone.

It was time to say good-bye. I was afraid to hug everyone for fear I would start crying. Why is not crying so important? I have since learned hugging people I care about is much more important than not crying. Such pain in leaving! We had shared our lives so deeply, but never acknowledging it. Colonel Girdner escorted me to the plane.

In Saigon I stayed at Dede's apartment. She had gone out on Leave.

The next day was Memorial Day back home. I remembered watching the parade last year walking down main street. Such a long time ago! So much had happened since then. I wanted my parents to know what I had learned and what I experienced, but how could I tell them? I never did!

My last day in Vietnam I finished processing and picked up tickets for Hong Kong, then on to Australia.

That last evening I sat up on the roof of the apartment building watching chopper gunships putting in air strikes a short distance away. I could not hear any sound coming from the explosions. I had heard about such strange acoustics before.

After an hour's delay, the plane lifted off the runway at Tan Son Nhut airport on June 1.

I checked into the Fortuna Hotel in Hong Kong. On a boat tour around the harbor, looking at the steep hillside, I wondered why all those buildings squeezed together hadn't fallen into the bay with a strong wind. After a tour of the city itself, I flew on to Sydney on June 5.

I had pictures with me that I had taken of the destruction in Phu Vinh that I hadn't wanted my parents to see until I was home. The customs officer looked through every one. I was the last to leave the airport.

On the way to the Canberra Oriental Hotel, I asked the cab driver how I could really see Australia, perhaps a sheep ranch I could visit. He told me MacDonald's ranch was family run and they take in guests.

That evening I came down to the hotel lounge to write home. Several people had gathered round the TV. The station interrupted to bring a special report: Bobby Kennedy had been shot and was dead. Anger rushed over me, "What is happening to my country?"

The next morning, I boarded the train for the seven-hour trip to Cowra. Mr. MacDonald met me at the station.

"We don't have any sheep right now. They have all been sold off for the winter, but we do have nine horses, two kangaroos, several chickens, and ducks."

"What beautiful country," I said as we rode along, "and how peaceful."

Mr. MacDonald continued, "My son and some of his friends are coming tomorrow from the University in Sydney for a few days."

Mrs. MacDonald met me at the door and escorted me into the living room where the other guests had gathered for tea and biscuits, along with two lovable Australian terriers I would enjoy, even though they ran the house!

Just after dark a car pulled in. Mr. and Mrs. Rushforth and their two daughters had come to stay.

After dinner, with everyone sitting round the fireplace and Mrs. MacDonald at the spinning wheel, working the wool, she asked me straight out, "How bad was it in Vietnam?"

The room fell silent! All eyes on me! Without thought nor hesitation, I blurted out, "We were surrounded at times."

Mrs. Rushforth came and sat next to me. "My husband was a POW of the Japanese. He said if he survived, he would do what he loves: to teach ceramics. So he got the education he needed to do just that."

Across the room I saw Mr. Rushforth had a sad understanding look about him.

Mrs. MacDonald crossed the room to the china cabinet. She reached in and brought out a very old bowl. "My brother was in North Africa during the war. He brought back this piece of pottery."

Mr. Rushforth came to her and carefully examining the bowl said, "This may be around a thousand years old."

He turned to me, "Would you like to look at it?"

"No, I'd be afraid I might drop it."

I could see the headlines all over Australia—"American nurse returning home from Vietnam dropped and broke a thousand-year-old bowl and is given life in prison."

After sunset it got really cold. The guests' rooms were in a built-on hallway a distance from the heat source of the fireplace and a huge cook stove in the kitchen. I had brought with me insulated pants and a top, which were a blessing.

I wrote home that night explaining some of the TET offensive. Now I wouldn't have to tell my parents face to face.

The land was covered with a heavy coating of frost glistening in the early-morning sun. Their son, with three of his friends, had gotten in sometime during the night, leaving one of their cars stuck in the mud that was now fixed solid in the frozen goo. Later, with increasing warmth, they were able to push it free, with great laughter!

Mr. and Mrs. Rushforth then invited me to their home overnight and then she would show me important sites. I agreed eagerly.

The MacDonalds' son and his friends invited me to come horseback riding with them. We rode to a cabin on the ranch. We laughed at anything and nothing. Everything was funny. They drew me into their friendship, unaware of their healing gift, though I was almost a decade older than they.

The next couple of days were much the same. Riding to the cabin. Trying to build a fire to make tea, all of us being quite inept arranging the wood in the fireplace—but always with laughter.

In the evenings we'd all go to the pub with Mr. and Mrs. MacDonald. Friendship, laughter, and darts trumped any drinking.

The last evening, after dinner, at 7:00 I rode with the students back to Sydney.

By the time we cleared the mountains, it was almost midnight. We stopped at a restaurant for coffee. Our unrestrained laughter continued, silly and loud to where I thought we might be kicked out.

They dropped me off at the hotel about 2 a.m. and were gone, never to see them again. I wondered if they knew how much they had helped me.

The next evening, I walked over to the university and found Mr. Rushforth absorbed in his ceramics class. I watched as he moved from student to student, touching each piece of work no matter how incongruously distorted it may be. I saw how this, for him, was healing from the agony and terror of a Japanese prison camp.

I had come early, so I walked around the campus until he had finished class. We arrived at his home around nine that evening. The living room had several shelves lining one wall filled with all colors, shapes, and textures of ceramics he had made.

Mrs. Rushforth brought in tea and biscuits as we talked about his work.

In the morning Mrs. Rushforth drove me around to different points of interest. We stopped at a particularly beautiful place, high up, overlooking the ocean. I thought, if I ever had to live in another country, it would be Australia. The kindness they all afforded to a stranger among them was truly extraordinary, to say the least.

Back in Sydney I visited an animal farm on an island, went through a museum, and, as always, shopped.

Now I was getting anxious to be on my way home!

June 15, I left Sydney for Los Angeles then on to Washington, D.C. The plane stopped in New Zealand and Samoa, then to Hawaii where I went through customs and was booked straight through to Washington with a four-hour layover in Los Angeles.

I arrived Sunday morning in D.C. Made my way to the hotel and called home. Then walked to the New York Avenue Presbyterian Church where Ginny and I had gone. I started walking back to the hotel but couldn't go any farther. I had no idea how long it had been since I last slept. I took a cab. I slept until 8 p.m., then called home again, and went back to bed and slept until 8 a.m. Now I was ready for the day-long paperwork and debriefing at State.

That evening, June 17, at 8:30 I touched down at the Syracuse airport and into the arms of my family.

Home and unaware! Left within me the pain of memory!
Then came grief!
And finally victory in Jesus!

> Brethren, I do not regard myself as having laid hold of it yet; but one thing I do: forgetting what lies behind and reaching forward to what lies ahead, I press on toward the goal for the prize of the upward call of God in Christ Jesus.
> —Philippians 3:13–14

> We have reached the end of the tunnel and there is no light there.
> —Walter Cronkite, CBS News 1975

Epilogue

Linda Beth Ellison

Linda became ill with symptoms of a headache, sore throat, stomachache, and general malaise without a fever. Dr. Dickstein examined her closely with lab tests, X-rays, and then put her on antibiotics.

The stomach pain increased, and she vomited. Dr. Dickstein notified Mr. Hayden, the deputy province advisor, who called the general. A helicopter medi-vac was called in at 11 p.m. Tuesday, August 6.

A four-vehicle escort took the Ellisons to the runway in Phu Vinh. Each vehicle illuminated the runway enough for the chopper to land. They flew on to Dong Tham Evac. Center in My Tho. The medical/surgical doctor thought Linda had pneumonia, and he put her on penicillin and streptomycin. Her breathing then became labored with a temperature that rose quickly to 104 degrees and brought on convulsions. Linda lost consciousness. A tracheotomy was done, but they lacked the equipment and medications there that she needed.

A helicopter was ready at 5:00 a.m. to take Linda to the Third Field Hospital in Saigon, but the battery was dead. Then another chopper was called in from Saigon, delaying treatment.

At the Third Field Hospital she was put on a ventilator, then a cut-down for fluids, a lumbar puncture, X-rays, more tests, and then into the ICU.

Paul and Eunice were given less than a 50-50 chance for Linda to live. She had near renal failure and was given little hope that she would not have extensive brain damage.

"At this time Paul and I had many opportunities to witness to those caring for Linda."

Eunice continued, "Just before noon on Monday the twelfth, her little heart stopped and she went to be with the Lord. Linda has given us five precious wonderful, happy years and we do not in any way question His wisdom or love. Perhaps the extra days of illness were permitted to give us time to adjust to a life without her. God is so good. She surely was a sweet, loving, little darling. I can imagine the joy she is experiencing as she investigates the inexhaustible wonders of heaven. Just imagine, all the living stories she is seeing and hearing there."

Linda died of encephalitis. She is buried in Moc Dinh Chi Cemetery near the International Church in Saigon.

Engraved in her tombstone is Zechariah 8:5: "And the streets of the city shall be full of boys and girls playing in the streets thereof."

THE ELLISON CHILDREN

Elaine was born in Bound Brook, New Jersey, in 1953. She became a K-12 teacher and taught grades K-5. Elaine had to retire early due to being diagnosed with multiple system atrophy/Parkinsonism in 2016. Her doctors attributed it to environmental exposure to Agent Orange.

Elaine and her family live in Washington State.

David was born in Phnom Penh, Cambodia, in 1955. He became an orthopedic surgeon specializing in hand surgery.

David and his family live in New York State.

Beau (Bobby) was born in Bangkok, Thailand, in 1958. He became a middle-school teacher. In their summers, Beau and his wife Mim, a school nurse, take mission trips to Zimbabwe to share the Good News of Jesus. Working alongside local Zimbabwe pastors, they reach out into remote areas, teaching in seminars.

Beau and his family live in California.

Linda was born in Saigon and in Saigon is where she left our world to "investigate the inexhaustible wonders of heaven with Jesus" (May 26, 1963 to August 12, 1968).

Acknowledgments

My lifelong friend since grade school, Yvonne "Vonnie" Abbey Pollock, after reading this manuscript expressed deep emotion in understanding as to why I had to write this story and what I experienced. I am grateful for her time spent in typing this work. How blessed I am for having had such friendship these many years.

Elaine Ellison Skene was very insightful in reading the manuscript and giving suggestions and corrections I needed in order to complete this work. Thank you, great friend.

I wish to thank Lydia Johnson Grandy, owner of Johnson Studio & Camera, for her help and expertise with this project. I deeply appreciate the time spent, my friend.

GLOSSARY

Agent Orange: Toxic Contaminant Herbicide Composed of 2,4-D and 2,4,5-T
ARVN: Army of the Republic of Vietnam (South Vietnam)
APC: Armored Personnel Carrier (U.S.)
Chinook: Army's Largest Supply and Transport Chopper
Chopper: Helicopter
CORDS: Civil Operations and Revolutionary Development Support
Gunship: Army's Primary Attack Helicopter called Cobra
Hemostat: A Surgical Clamp, Usually Used to Clamp Bleeders
IVS: International Voluntary in Service (U.S. Civilian Volunteers)
LST: Landing Ship Transport (U.S. Navy)
LZ: Landing Zone
MACV: Military Assistance Command, Vietnam
Milphap: American Medical Team in Provincial Hospitals
NVA: North Vietnamese Army
PBR Boat: Patrol Boat River, used in the Mekong Delta
Tin-Lanh Church: Means Good News
USAID: Agency for International Development (AID)
VC: Viet Cong, communists in South Vietnam

About the Author

Nancy Churchill, shortly after coming home from Vietnam, went to Bible college. She continued to work as a nurse, enjoying vacations in the Adirondack Mountains. Now retired, she has had time to attend many Bible conferences. Nancy lives in upstate New York.

CPSIA information can be obtained
at www.ICGtesting.com
Printed in the USA
LVHW071402020320
648710LV00064B/3410